Becoming Jesus' Prayer

Becoming Jesus' Prayer

Transforming Your Life Through the Lord's Prayer

Gregory V. Palmer

Cindy M. McCalmont,

Brian K. Milford

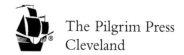

The Pilgrim Press
Cleveland

The Pilgrim Press
700 Prospect Avenue
Cleveland, Ohio 44115-1100
thepilgrimpress.com

Printed in the United States of America on acid-free paper

15 14 13 12 11   8 7 6 5

Library of Congress Cataloging-in-Publication Data

Palmer, Gregory V., 1954-
    Becoming Jesus' prayer : transforming your life through the Lord's prayer/
    Gregory Palmer, Cindy McCalmont, Brian Milford.
       p.   cm.
    Includes bibliographical references.
    ISBN 0-8298-1707-7
    1. Lord's prayer. 2. Spiritual life—Christianity. 3. Christian life.
    I. McCalmont, Cindy (Cindy M.) 1963– II. Milford, Brian (Brian K.),
    1959– III. Title.
  BV230.P35 2005
  226.9'606—dc22   2005028972

ISBN 13 : 978-0-8298-1707-2
ISBN 10 : 0-8298-1707-7

~ Contents

~ Acknowledgments

This book would not be in your hands without:

+ All among us who are becoming Jesus' Prayer

+ The prayerful responses of Iowa United Methodists who shared their experiences and reflections on Jesus' Prayer

+ Genny Yarne, head of reference, Kirkwood Community College, Cedar Rapids, Iowa, for her tireless research assistance

~ Introduction

OVER THE LAST SEVERAL YEARS in the body of Christ, we have observed a faddish fascination—if not a down right craze on the part of some Christians—to find just the right incantation to bring God's blessing to their lives. No doubt you have observed this too. It can be observed or experienced in various churches, many of which are known because of the wide net that they cast through television and cable broadcasting. Some of these incantations, which masquerade as prayer, are known to us because they have become quite popular through small devotional books that have swept the land.

Obviously we cannot, nor should we judge the intentions or motivations of preachers and authors who have invited God's people to pray, to pray in certain ways let alone seek God's blessing for their lives. In fact it occurs to us that perhaps certain widely popular practices of prayer have grabbed center stage because they address a profound and deep hunger for God and for meaningful ways to commune with God. Our bias is that God's people in Christ have a time honored and life tested vocabulary for praying. This vocabulary has served us well, whether in the quiet of our own devotions, in small groups, or in public worship. The concern that we have about much of what we observe in the prayer life of some Christians, particularly in the Western world, is that it seems so self-indulgent and nationalistic.

When all is said and done, only God can meaningfully address our deepest hungers. We only really know God in relationship. Our relationship with God grows through prayer—meaningful, ongoing engagement with God. God's Son and our Savior, Jesus the Christ, led a life of prayer, and by precept and example, invites his followers in every age to do likewise.

In Luke 11:1–2 we find these words: "He was praying in a certain place, and after he had finished, one of his disciples said to him, 'Lord, teach us to pray, as John taught his disciples.' 'He said to them, When you pray, say....'"

So this study is offered not because the church or the world needs another study, much less another study on the Lord's Prayer. If you choose to proceed beyond this introduction, you will discover that Becoming Jesus' Prayer: Transforming Your Life through the Lord's Prayer is not offered to give you more information; rather, it is an invitation to transformation. As you make your way through this material, you will be encouraged to find your home in this prayer and to let the Lord's Prayer live in you. You will hear a clear and unambiguous invitation to be changed, to become the prayer.

This book is an invitation to breathe this prayer in community with others. In order for this call to prayer to connect with you, we were and are convinced that we need to hear the stories of other pilgrims on the journey. In hearing the stories of colleagues in faith, we believe that we find the capacity to tell our own stories and name our experiences in the light and countenance of the God who came among us as one of us. We are so grateful to the saints who have been courageous enough to share their stories and their experience with the prayer that Jesus taught.

It has been a gift of enormous proportions to work so closely in community on this project that was birthed to be a gift to our communion and judicatory. We have met, talked, laughed, cried, sung and prayed together. We have pushed and prodded each other. We have critiqued one another's thinking and parsed each others writing. We have experienced the church at its best and found great joy in noting the ties that bind us in Christian unity. We have anguished over the fissures in the body of Christ, particularly those that seem to invite bad behavior toward colleagues in Christ and mute our witness to the world. We have had more fun together than we perhaps deserve as we have opened ourselves to becoming Jesus' prayer.

Our work together has reminded us again and again that life in Christ—its challenges not withstanding—is a gift from God's generous heart.

Every session begins with a story, offers theological reflection and gives suggestions for conversation, prayer, worship and action. We have attempted to prepare this guide with a wide and diverse audience in mind. Feel free to supplement it with other resources. Don't try to go it alone. This study presumes life in community. The Lord's Prayer is a prayer for the community. Most of all pray. Pray this prayer with others. Reflect on what you are praying and saying. Listen to others. Let the prayer wash over you until you are comforted, convicted and converted. Pray it until you experience joy and sorrow. Pray it humbly. Pray it boldly. Pray until Jesus' Prayer transforms you. Pray it as long as you have life and breath.

"For the whole of our life to our death, each of us should be, and continue to become, a commentary on the Lord's Prayer." (The Reverend Bernard Häring).*

Yearning to become Jesus' prayer,
GREGORY V. PALMER
CINDY MCCALMONT
BRIAN MILFORD

†Epiphany 2006

*Bernard Häring, *Our Father* (Winona, Mn.: St. Mary's Press, 1995), 7.

~ LEADER'S GUIDE

A S THE LEADER FOR THIS STUDY, your role is one of a group facilitator and guide rather than a lecturer or teacher. That's because the study is not informational in nature but transformational. In other words, the goal of the study is that participants would be changed as they pray, study, practice, and journey together through this very familiar prayer. Thus, it is important that you are a friend and companion through this exploration of Jesus' Prayer and help establish an atmosphere of trust, openness, and encouragement.

The chapters are intended to be used in a 45–75-minute session. They are not designed to go week-by-week through the verses, nor are they intellectual comparisons of the variations of the prayer in scripture and in our denominations. In addition, they are not presented in a "step-by-step" format. Instead, the expectation is that you as leader will help shape the session for your particular situation. Here are two examples of structures you might use for the study, with options to consider:

PLAN 1

(assumes the participants read and reflect on the material in advance)

GATHERING THE COMMUNITY (10–15 MIN.)

+ Open with a hymn or two suggested by this study.

+ Have a volunteer read one of the prayers included either in the theological reflection or in the ideas for personal and corporate prayer.

+ Spend a few minutes "checking in" with one another, sharing joys and concerns, etc.

THE COMMUNITY EXPLORES (20–30 MIN.)

+ Talk about the week's readings. (On week 1, you will need to take time to read these together.)

+ Answer the Topics for Discussion, adding your own as the conversation allows.

+ Discuss any issues and questions that individuals wrote down during their personal study and journaling.

THE COMMUNITY REFLECTS (10–20 MIN.)

+ Engage in the corporate prayer suggestions, emphasizing that these are various ways of praying together.

+ Spend some time in silence, increasing the number of minutes each week.

+ Give the class members 5–10 minutes to reflect in their journals; allow time for those who are willing to share part or all of their writing.

THE COMMUNITY IS SENT OUT (5–10 MIN.)

+ Pray Jesus' Prayer as a community.
+ Close with another appropriate prayer.
+ Sing one of the other suggested hymns.

PLAN 2

(assumes most participants will read the material during the session)

GATHERING (5–10 MIN.)

+ Open with a hymn or two suggested by this study.
+ Have a volunteer read one of the suggested prayers.
+ Spend a few minutes "checking in" with one another and reviewing insights from or since the last session.

READ AND RESPOND (25–35 MIN.)

+ Have one individual read the opening story aloud as others listen or follow along. Preferably, ask that person in advance of the study so that they can practice reading it with emotion and clarity.
+ Share reactions to the story.

+ Read the theological reflection. You might do this silently, or you could have different individuals read a paragraph at a time.

+ Talk about portions of the theological reflection, either in small groups or periodically as the material is read.

Go Deeper (10–20 min.)

+ Answer the Topics for Discussion, adding your own as necessary.

+ As a class, choose one of the corporate prayer suggestions.

Reentering the World (5–10 min.)

+ Sing one of the suggested hymns.

+ Reflect together on ways to bring the prayer to life during the coming week.

+ Pray Jesus' Prayer as a community.

Ideally, participants would read and reflect on the material in advance of each discussion. That way you'll have far more time for in-depth exploration of the week's material. Regardless of the approach you use, try to experience the fullness and diversity of options for praying. There are many ways to pray, and people learn them by practicing them.

Remember, too, that individuals learn in many ways. Some people in your group may enjoy silence and journaling, others will respond best to music or movement, and some may be most energized by discussing the ways their life is their prayer. They probably don't learn exactly the way you do. Be sure that you try a variety of ways to engage the scripture—visually, orally, aurally, logically, kinesthetically, interpersonally, and so on. The more variety you can bring to the study, the more participants will gain from it.

Four Versions of Jesus' Prayer

Our Father, who art in heaven, hallowed be thy name.
Thy kingdom come. Thy will be done on earth as it is in
heaven.
Give us this day our daily bread. And forgive us our
trespasses, as we forgive those who
trespass against us.
And lead us not into temptation, but deliver us from evil.
For thine is the kingdom, and the power, and the glory,
for ever and ever.
Amen.

Our Father, who art in heaven, hallowed be thy name.
Thy kingdom come. Thy will be done on earth as it is in
heaven.

Give us this day our daily bread.
And forgive us our debts, as we forgive our debtors.
And lead us not into temptation, but deliver us from evil.
For thine is the kingdom, and the power, and the glory for ever.
Amen.

Our Father in heaven, hallowed be your name, your kingdom come, your will be done, on earth as in heaven.
Give us today our daily bread. Forgive us our sins as we forgive those who sin against us.
Save us from the time of trial and deliver us from evil.
For the kingdom, the power, and the glory are yours now and for ever.
Amen.

Our Father-Mother, who is in the heavens, may your name be made holy.
May your dominion come, may your will be done, on earth as it is in heaven.
Give us today the bread we need;
and forgive us our debts, as we have forgiven our debtors;
and do not put us to the test, but rescue us from evil.
For yours is the dominion, and the power, and the glory forever.
Amen.

from the *New Century Hymnal,* The United Church of Christ

CHAPTER ONE

~ JESUS' PRAYER OPENS US TO THE HOLY

S HE SAT QUIETLY, PATIENTLY. Her clothes were simple. Her fresh-scrubbed skin was untouched by cosmetics or perfumes, yet emanated a sweetness that puzzled me. I watched her with all the wisdom of my eight-year-old mind. I knew she was alone with a large family, in a time when that was not common. I knew that she was very poor and that in her home she swept dirt. And I knew that something drew me to her. I chose to sit beside her in the pew that Sunday morning. And something made me watch.

Then came the part of worship I had been waiting for. My class had just completed our memorization of Jesus' Prayer. So here was my chance. I had been waiting all week. Finally, I could say it all the way through without looking, just like the grown-ups around me. I began to recite, with boisterous enthusiasm: "Our Father, who art . . ." But I stopped midword and held my breath. I listened. I peeked. Mrs. M. was saying those same words, but her voice, her face, her very being weren't just reciting. These age-old words memorized by millions and repeated by that number around the world every week weren't words. They were a prayer—a living, breathing conversation with our God.[1]

THEOLOGICAL REFLECTION

"Saying one's prayers is not the same as praying."[2] With this one sentence, a much beloved character in children's literature, Anne of Green Gables, makes plain the trouble that we have with the prayer that Jesus taught us. We can say the prayer, reciting the memorized phrases with ease. The question is: Can we pray it?

In the earliest days of Christianity, this prayer was considered such a treasure that people had to go through three years of training and preparation before they could be entrusted with the sacred words.[3] Now we casually teach the prayer to our children and mindlessly mouth it in worship. In our well-meaning and sincere efforts to memorize the prayer, we have lost its wild power. Intended by Jesus to be a prayer that helps us to soar, the prayer has become so familiar and so domesticated that we barely pay attention. Jesus' Prayer has had its wings clipped.

In the liturgy for Holy Communion, however, we are reminded how important this prayer really is. In the context of communion, this is a prayer that prepares us to receive the presence of Christ into our bodies; it prepares us as a community of faith to become Christ's body. The irony is that these ordinary sentences point to the extraordinary. These seemingly perfunctory phrases are alive with the mystery and miracle of our faith. If we allow it, Jesus' Prayer can open us to the holy.

As Richard Foster has written: "Real prayer comes not from gritting our teeth but from falling in love."[4] Jesus taught the disciples that prayer is not merely about the reciting of religious words, the self-satisfied completion of our spiritual duty. The Pharisees did that. True prayer is about allowing ourselves to fall in love with God. True prayer is about being carried away by the Spirit. True prayer is about having the heart of Christ.

The Reverend Hal Green describes a vision that he had while praying:

Once in prayer, I had an experience of interconnection with Jesus, heart to heart, soul to soul. It began when I sensed Christ drawing near to me with an unexpected but desired directness, inviting me to intimacy. As Christ drew nearer, my heart grew warmer, seeming to expand. I realized that my heart, aflame but not burning up, was no longer my heart alone; the boundaries between my heart and the heart of Jesus had dissolved, so I could not separate the one from the other. Then a rainbow appeared between us, seeable not with eyes of the head, but with eyes of the heart. One base of the rainbow was planted deeply in Christ's heart, the other in my heart. For the full length of the arc, for the fleeting life of our rainbow, Jesus and I were one. In a mutuality beyond words, it was as if I were knowing as I was being known, loving as I was being loved. Heaven is being heart to heart with Christ.[5]

You don't have to have visions to understand that Jesus' Prayer can bring us heart to heart with Christ—not just in what we see in our minds but in what we do with our lives. When we allow this prayer to open us to the holy, boundaries between heaven and earth dissolve. We know union with God and kinship with one another.

Praying Jesus' Prayer, however, may not always be done with hands folded and heads bowed. We can pray the prayer as we engage in a task that is done for others. At the University of Iowa, students have been praying with knitting needles and skeins of yarn. Each weekday 150 persons line up for a free lunch program that is housed in a local church building. One of the university students saw that the people were cold as they waited outside for their meals, so she got the idea of knitting them scarves as Christmas presents. Between tests and papers, she knitted and taught her friends to knit. Other people heard about the project and donated yarn and volunteered to help make the scarves. With each row of stitches, these students prayed their intercessions for those who are in great need of daily bread. They prayed for God's will to be done, for God's reign to come. In Iowa City, God's reign has been emerging one scarf at a time. God's children are knitted together in love.

Walt Whitman wrote that we must help one another to wipe the gum from our eyes and to dress ourselves for the dazzle of the light.[6] This prayer is a summons to wake up from our spiritual complacency and to meet the living Christ. Jesus' Prayer can open us to the holy everywhere—in corporate worship and solitary contemplation, in soup kitchen lines and university classrooms, in the stranger on the street and the neighbor next door. Our God in heaven is intimate in our lives and in our world, but we won't be able to see the splendor of the light unless we pray, unless we seek to be heart to heart with Christ.

TOPICS FOR DISCUSSION

Share an early memory of Jesus' Prayer. How long have you known it?

What has this prayer taught you about who God is? Use a dictionary or a Bible dictionary to explore the words "hallowed" and "holy." What do they add to your understanding of God?

The gospels tell us that Jesus often drew apart to pray. How do you imagine Jesus praying?

What about prayer is most joyful for you? What about prayer causes you to struggle? Where do you find joy and struggle in the praying of Jesus' Prayer?

The Reverend Hal Green shared an extraordinary experience of God that he had in prayer. Talk about your most extraordinary experience of God.

PRAYER AT HOME THIS WEEK

Pray Jesus' Prayer every day for the next week. Tape a copy of it to your bathroom mirror. Place it on your kitchen table. Make the prayer the screen saver on your computer. Attach it to the visor in your car. Live with the prayer for the next seven days. Let the words saturate your mind and heart.

Start a journal to accompany you during this study. Begin by writing about one of the following comments:

+ Imagine that you are one of the disciples asking Jesus to teach you how to pray. Describe the scene.

+ Make a list of the different ways that people can pray. Which methods are best for you?

+ Write about a time when corporate prayer was meaningful for you.

+ Write about a time when solitary prayer touched your spirit.

+ The Quaker theologian Thomas Kelly said that "prayer is to be invaded to the depths of one's being by God's presence."[7] What do you think Kelly meant?

+ Write a prayer that expresses the longings of your heart.

Read and meditate on the next section of this study, "Jesus' Prayer Teaches the Faith."

CORPORATE PRAYER

These suggestions are appropriate for your study group and/or for worship services in your congregation.

Pray Jesus' Prayer together more slowly than usual, pausing between the phrases.

Sing the West Indian version of the prayer.[8]

Read the different versions of Jesus' Prayer. Allow for a time of silence between the reading of each one.

HYMN SUGGESTIONS

Please select similar hymns or other songs that may be found in your denominational hymn book.

1. "O Jesus I Have Promised"[9]

2. "Dear God Embracing Humankind" (also known as "Dear Lord and Father of Mankind")[10]

3. "As the Deer"[11]

4. "Open Our Eyes"[12]

CHAPTER TWO

~ JESUS' PRAYER TEACHES THE FAITH

IT WAS A "REGULAR" Sunday in worship. The pastor was present, warmly greeting the congregation as they arrived. The choir shared a beautiful, moving anthem, as always. No member was experiencing a health crisis. No noticeable mistakes were in the bulletin. We moved through worship with celebration and caring. At the end of a thoughtful pastoral prayer, we began, as usual, the congregational rendering of Jesus' Prayer. Suddenly the clear voice of a three year old rang out. He had just learned this prayer and was earnestly praying. A hush settled over the congregation. But we became fearful that he would quit praying if we quit praying, so our voices immediately joined back in the congregational prayer. We continued quietly as we strained to hear this young child in his fervent prayer. The service could have ended then for we had all worshiped. God was there with that child and we all knew it. The memory of that young voice in prayer still echoes in my heart.[1]

THEOLOGICAL REFLECTION

"Teach us to pray," the disciples implored Jesus.[2] And Jesus responded not by teaching them how to pray but by giving them a prayer that would teach them faith. Jesus gave the disciples both a prayer and a pattern for prayer.

Those who have struggled with discipleship know that it is impossible to simply "study" what it means to follow Jesus without actually taking the first step. Neither can we "study" Jesus' Prayer without actually praying it. We learn to pray by praying. We learn to pray this prayer by allowing its words to become so much a part of who we are that the words of the prayer become our words. A young voice earnestly praying the words, fervently saying them out loud in worship, is an inspiration to all of us because that young boy is struggling to make this prayer his very own conversation with God. And as we continue on that journey, Jesus' Prayer has the ability to make an impact on our lives and instruct us in the faith as we allow its words to become our words. For some of us, we do not remember a time when we did not know this prayer. For others, one of the first steps of discipleship involved learning the words of the prayer.

The words we pray in Jesus' Prayer embody the essential elements of our faith. Tertullian, an early Christian writer from North Africa, described Jesus' Prayer as being "an epitome of the whole Gospel."[3] This brief summary of the Gospel of Jesus Christ conveys to us what it means to be a faithful disciple of Jesus. It calls us to the essence of our faith in the same way that Deuteronomy 6:4–5 describes the essence of the covenant between God and God's people, Israel: "Hear, O Israel: the Lord is your God, the Lord alone. You shall love the Lord your God with all your heart, and with all your soul, and with all your might." Those verses summarized the relationship between God and the people. The people were instructed to teach those words to their children, place them on their doorposts, and keep them in their hearts. In a similar way, Jesus' Prayer summarizes what it means to be faithful.

Maureen Williams remembers the day she was approached by a fellow in need of food on the streets of Omaha, Nabraska. She describes a feeling of self-righteousness as she told the drunken homeless man that she couldn't give him any money for food. The next time she prayed the words "thy kingdom come, thy will be done," she was confronted. "Jesus' Prayer keeps reminding me that to be a Christian I must continue to seek to be like Christ and love my neighbor."[4]

A retired physician writes, "I've attended many Alcoholics Anonymous meetings, and we end those meetings holding hands in a circle reciting Jesus' Prayer together. Many seeds are planted in the unbeliever through the words of the prayer."[5]

Those who join our churches with no previous

Christian background are hungry to learn about our faith. Those of us who have been part of the faith for a long time tend to forget that those who are new to Christianity are looking for some understanding of what is essential. Jesus' Prayer is a tool to teach what faithful discipleship involves. The prayer teaches us to honor God as we work for God's realm to come on earth as in heaven. We are taught that forgiveness lies at the heart of what it means to be faithful and that God offers deliverance from evil. We are taught to rely upon God's ability to sustain us as we pray for our daily bread. We are taught that ultimately God is in charge and that true power and glory are found in relationship with God.

As we pray the prayer together, we are called and challenged to grow in our faith. The phrases of the prayer, spoken by a recovering alcoholic, a self-righteous Christian, or a three year old just learning the words, are empowered by the Holy Spirit to instruct our lives, both corporate and personal, and call us to a deeper faith.

TOPICS FOR DISCUSSION

What has Jesus' Prayer taught you about what it means to follow in the way of Christ?

Talk about significant experiences that continue to teach you what it means to be a person of faith.

Make a list of some of the phrases or passages in the Bible that you might use to summarize the Christian faith (e.g., "Love the Lord Your God with all your heart, and with all your soul, and with all your strength, and with all your mind, and your neighbor as yourself"[6]). Why do you think Tertullian referred to Jesus' Prayer as "an epitome of the whole gospel"?

Break into small groups and pass out study Bibles, commentaries, and resources on Jesus' Prayer. Give each group a phrase of the prayer to study, and ask them to spend 5–10 minutes learning more about it. Ask the groups to pay special attention to what the phrases teach us about our Christian faith. Bring the groups back together and have an individual from each group summarize what they have learned.

How might Jesus' Prayer be useful in teaching discipleship to someone who is new to the faith? Role play a conversation between a disciple and someone who is trying to learn what discipleship means using this prayer as a model for teaching.

PRAYER AT HOME THIS WEEK

Teach Jesus' Prayer to someone who does not know it, or have a conversation with someone about what this prayer teaches us about our faith.

Continue to reflect on Jesus' Prayer in your journal. The following questions might be helpful in guiding your thoughts:

+ List what the prayer teaches you about following Jesus.

+ Imagine yourself speaking to someone who is trying to understand what it means to be a Christian. How could this prayer be helpful in teaching them what discipleship means?

+ Write about a time when Jesus' Prayer reminded you of what you must do in a specific situation as a follower of Christ.

Read and meditate on the next section of this study, "Jesus' Prayer Calls us to Forgiveness."

CORPORATE PRAYER

Invite a child to pray Jesus' Prayer on behalf of the group or congregation during this next week.

Pray together "The Prayer of Ignatius of Loyola."[7]

Sing together "What Wondrous Love is This"[8] or "They'll Know We are Christians by Our Love."[9]

HYMN SUGGESTIONS

"Seek ye First"[10]

"Lord I Want to Be a Christian"[11]

"Gather Us In"[12]

CHAPTER THREE

~ JESUS' PRAYER CALLS US TO FORGIVENESS

O N JANUARY 31, 1987, my sixteen-year-old son, Jeffrey Phillip Marvin, died. The line from Jesus' Prayer—"forgive us our trespasses as we forgive those who trespass against us"—kept coming to my mind. I was so sad. It was reported that the boy driving the car that Jeff rode in was driving partly in the ditch at a high rate of speed. I thought I should be filled with anger, much anger. I prayed and prayed.

Tragedy continued to happen in our small town. My husband's principal at school lost his daughter in a car accident after she lost control of her car. My husband and I felt we should attend the funeral. However, it was just a few months after Jeff left us, and we knew it was going to be so difficult. Yet, we remembered how the people who supported us and came to Jeff's funeral helped so much.

We arrived to a full church. There was just one part of a pew left for us in the small balcony. As I entered, I was seated next to the mother of the young man who drove the car that Jeff had been riding in. *Our family sat right next to him and his family at this funeral.*

My mind was full of grief as I sat at this funeral, but I knew only God would place me in this position. It was a position of two families brought together side by side. I was sitting next to the mother of this boy. As we sat, I could sense the colors of the stained-glass window behind us. I could feel the tension in this other mother knowing of her pain for her son as well as for us. As we sat through the funeral, I could feel the hurt in her heart. I knew God was with me as I reached over and took her hand in mine. I hugged her as we shared quiet words. God led me to have the strength to take her hand and give her comfort, one mother to another.[1]

THEOLOGICAL REFLECTION

The theologian John Koenig defines forgiveness this way: "Forgiveness turns out not to be a work or a pronouncement but a discovery that grows out of our realization that we and the people from whom we are estranged are not very different after all."[2] Forgiveness begins with an awareness of our shared humanity, a recognition of the tremendous capacity that we have to both destroy and bless one another. The apostle Paul understood the complexity of our human nature—how we struggle to make the right choices, and how we sometimes do the very thing we despise: "For I do not do the good I want, but

the evil I do not want is what I do."[3] If we can acknowl-
edge the potential that we have for harming others, then
we can have more compassion for those who hurt us.

This honest self-appraisal can also enable us to see our
need for interior cleansing. Even as we organize cup-
boards and wash windows in our homes, we are called
upon to sort through and clean our hearts. An African
schoolgirl described this need for cleaning when she
prayed: "O Thou great Chief, light a candle in my heart,
that I may see what is therein and sweep the rubbish from
thy dwelling place."[4] When we forgive, we are cleaning
our hearts of the clutter of anger and resentment. We are
washing away the stains of bitterness.

Jesus gives us the ultimate model for forgiveness. In the
Gospel of Luke, we are told that Jesus forgave, even as he
was being crucified. "Father, forgive them for they know
not what they are doing," Jesus prayed from the cross.[5]
Mocked and brutally tortured, still Jesus did not give in to
hatred. For Jesus, forgiveness wasn't something he did; forgiveness was who he was, how he looked on the world. As
one who sought to live in the likeness of Christ, Martin
Luther King, Jr., put it well when he said: "Forgiveness
isn't an occasional act; it is a permanent attitude."[6]

Forgiveness is not just an individual attitude; it is to be
the posture of our churches as well. In September of
2000, a church in Iowa was burned to the ground by an

arsonist. In the weeks and months that followed, the congregation had to wrestle with how to forgive the person who destroyed their 107-year-old church. On behalf of the congregation, the pastor of Farmers Chapel, the Reverend Ted Lyddon Hatten, wrote an open letter to the unknown arsonist and had it printed in the local newspaper, *The Record Herald*. The entire letter is included in Appendix 1 of this study, but the letter concluded with this invitation to the arsonist:

Our worship time is 9:00 AM every Sunday. I tell you this because I want you to know that you are invited. In fact, we even plan to reserve a seat just for you. Our faith has a lot to say about forgiveness. Every Sunday we ask God to forgive our sins but only as we have forgiven those who have sinned against us. That would be you. So if you would join us for worship, we could practice this kind of forgiveness face to face. I say "practice" for a reason. I don't expect us to get it right the first or even the second time. Of course we'll continue to work to forgive you even if you decline our invitation to worship. Forgiveness is the cornerstone of the faith we have inherited. Some people think it is impossible. They may be right. I only know that we have to try. Our forgiveness of you is tied to God's forgiveness of us. We can't receive something we are not willing to give to others.

So you see, if we harbor hatred for you in our hearts, we harbor the smoldering ashes of your arson. If we cling to bitterness, we fan the embers of your violent act. If we fantasize about revenge, we rekindle a destructive flame that will consume us. Forgiveness may indeed be impossible, but for us it is not optional.[7]

Forgiveness doesn't come easily. We must seek God's help as we work toward transforming our clenched fist into an open hand. We must pray for the Spirit's guidance as we attempt to liberate our hearts from the anger that will destroy us.

Archbishop Desmond Tutu was the chair of the Truth and Reconciliation Commission in South Africa. Through his leadership, the nation was able to both name the horrendous violence that people had inflicted on one another and at the same time retain a sense of hope that reconciliation was possible. In the process of bringing healing to South Africa, Tutu spoke profound words when he said that "there is no future without forgiveness."[8] We have no future if we cannot move toward reconciliation. We have no future if we cannot take seriously the call of our faith to forgive.

Farmers Chapel United Methodist Church has been rebuilt, and the focal point in the new sanctuary is a large cross that is mounted over the altar. The cross that the congregation chose isn't silver or gold. The cross isn't a mosaic of brightly colored panes of glass. The cross in Farmers Chapel is made from the charred wood of their former sanctuary. The cross has been constructed from the few blackened timbers that remained after the fire. Every Sunday morning now, the congregation worships with a visual reminder of the arsonist's act, but more than that, every Sunday morning they worship with the assurance that life comes out of death, that hope emerges from desolation. Farmers Chapel has it right: The cross of Christ is a summons to celebrate and to share the abundant forgiveness of our God.

TOPICS FOR DISCUSSION

Discuss the Reverend Ted Lyddon Hatten's statement:

> "Forgiveness may indeed be impossible, but for us it is not optional." When has your church experienced an opportunity for forgiveness? What happened and why?

Respond to the following prayer written by an unknown prisoner in Ravensbruck Concentration Camp:

> O Lord, remember not only the men and women of good will, but also those of ill will. But do not remember all the suffering they have inflicted on

us; remember the fruits we have bought, thanks to this suffering—our comradeship, our loyalty, our humility, our courage, our generosity, the greatness of heart which has grown out of all this, and when they come to judgment let the fruits which we have borne be their forgiveness. Amen.[9]

Look at a recent newspaper and make a list of the top stories. What would forgiveness look like if it were lived out in the events of our day?

Describe a scene from a movie that has to do with the theme of forgiveness. What is the message about forgiveness? (If the leader has time before this session, he or she could choose a movie clip to show to the group. Some movies that might work include: *Dead Man Walking, Les Miserables, My Best Friend's Wedding, The Spitfire Grill, The Mission, Mission Impossible 2.*)

Talk about the word "as" in the phrase "as we forgive…." One way to translate the phrase is "in the same manner as." What difference does it make how you understand that one little word?

PRAYER AT HOME THIS WEEK

C. S. Lewis wrote about a practice of prayer that he called

festooning.[10] In a familiar prayer like Jesus' Prayer, Lewis prayed it phrase by phrase, elaborating his thoughts and feelings. Pray Jesus' Prayer in this way for the next seven days. Pause after each phrase and include your own petitions.

Research the work of the Truth and Reconciliation Commission in South Africa. Pray intercessions for parts of our world that you think are most in need of truth and reconciliation today.

Topics for journaling:

+ What is your favorite story about forgiveness in the Bible? Why does this story speak to you?

+ Write about a time when you were forgiven. Include as much detail as possible about the experience.

+ "As we forgive those who trespass against us…." Who do you need to forgive? What are some steps that you might take to move toward forgiving?

+ Write about ways that your church may need to forgive or to be forgiven.

+ You are describing forgiveness to a five-year-old child. What do you say?

Read and meditate on the next section of this study, "Jesus' Prayer Brings Us Peace."

CORPORATE PRAYER

Use Jean Humphrey's *Jesus' Prayer in Hymns* found in Appendix 2. Read a phrase of Jesus' Prayer and then sing the accompanying hymn stanzas.

Sing "The Lord's Prayer."[11]

HYMN SUGGESTIONS

1. "Forgive Our Sins As We Forgive"[12]

2. "Let Us Break Bread Together"[13]

3. "Here, O My Lord, I See Thee"[14]

CHAPTER FOUR

~ JESUS' PRAYER BRINGS US PEACE

MANY YEARS AGO I WAS TAKING Clinical Pastoral Education at a hospital. I was on call one night and the pager rang at about 3:00 AM. I quickly dressed and went up to the nurses' station. They directed me to a room where a man was dying. He was greatly agitated and was moving all over the bed. After I introduced myself, he immediately requested prayer. I prayed Jesus' Prayer.

After the prayer was completed, a great calm came upon him. His transformation from anxiety to peace remains a mystery to me, but I credit the presence of almighty God and the great prayer taught to us by Jesus.[1]

THEOLOGICAL REFLECTION

Over and over again, people report that Jesus' Prayer brings them peace. From teenagers to senior citizens, the message is the same: The familiar cadence of this prayer gives solace and comfort. One high school student says that when she thinks of Jesus' Prayer, she imagines herself under a night sky filled with stars with God's peace over her.[2] A seminary student writes that praying this prayer in a new church touched her deeply at a time when she felt homesick and alone.[3] A senior citizen says that he prays Jesus' Prayer every night as he prepares to sleep, allowing the words of the prayer to travel through his mind like a gentle breeze.[4] The testimony of generations of Christians is in agreement. In sixty-eight words, Jesus' prayer centers us, connects us, calms us.

The promise of our faith isn't that our lives will be easy. We may know lonely days and sleepless nights. We may face crises in our health, our finances, and our relationships. We may see violence explode down the street and around the globe. Sometimes our fears, griefs, and longings will mass into overwhelming waves of sadness. But Jesus steadies the boat, speaking to our hearts: "Peace, be still."[5]

One woman describes how late one evening she learned that her grandfather had died. Unable to sleep, she prayed and sang Jesus' Prayer again and again. Mary says that the prayer was like a healing balm—giving her rest even though she wasn't sleeping, filling her with love and calm. She writes: "Every word of the prayer kept me company that night while I grieved my grandfather's death."[6] Mary puts it well. Jesus' Prayer can keep us company. These words that have been on the lips of Christians for nearly two millennia are an assurance that we are not alone in the struggles in our lives.

We would be in error, however, if we only spoke of Jesus' Prayer in relationship to our own personal peace. This prayer brings us peace in order that we might offer peace. Yet in the aftermath of September 11th, praying these all-too-familiar words may seem a naïve and hopeless response. In the midst of an agonizing war in Iraq and a devastating hurricane in the Mississippi delta, engaging in the repetition of a memorized prayer may seem ineffectual and meaningless. What difference can this prayer possibly make to a world terrorized by hijacked planes, suicide bombers, and the brutal assault of a hurricane? How can these phrases combat violence when towers come crashing down, bombs rain from the sky, and cities are laid waste by a storm?

As the Reverend David Beneke prayed after September 11th, "God is our tower of strength."[7] Jesus' Prayer reminds us that even though the earth may shake and the mountains fall into the sea, still the dominion, the power, and the glory belong to God. No matter what happens, we can live lives of confidence. We can have the courage to meet violence with compassion. We can take the risk of responding to our enemies with forgiveness.

As the crucifixion drew near, Jesus sought to prepare his disciples for the difficult days to come: "Peace I leave with you; my peace I give to you. I do not give to you as the world gives."[8] The peace of our faith is not the easy, happily-ever-after sentiment that we can find on greeting cards and television shows. Christ's peace doesn't curl up on the sofa or put its legs up in the La-Z-Boy. This is a peace that makes its way up Calvary's cross and down into the rubble in lower Manhattan, Baghdad, and New Orleans. This is a peace that travels to struggling family farms and crowded homeless shelters. Christ's peace doesn't protect itself from tragedy, pain, and suffering. With arms extended on the cross, Christ offers peace that reaches out to embrace the world.

As Christians, we can't live in a climate-controlled environment of tranquility. One lifelong Christian says that he used to hear his elders say, "If you want to be a person of faith, you gotta' be dug up."[9] We are so deeply rooted in our own wants that even our desire for personal peace can keep us self-absorbed. We gotta' be dug up. We need God to turn over the soil of our hearts. A prayer from the Church Missionary Society in Singapore echoes this understanding that true and lasting peace emerges from some personal discomfort:

> God stir the soil
> Run the ploughshare deep,
> Cut the furrows round and round,
> Overturn the hard, dry ground,
> Spare no strength nor toil,

Even though I weep.
In the loose, fresh mangled earth
Sow new seed.
Free of withered vine and weed
Bring fair flowers to birth. Amen.[10]

Jesus' Prayer brings us peace—but a peace that is beyond all understanding. When we are truly praying as Jesus prayed, we will experience both comfort and discomfort. We will be dug up, and we will be planted. We will know peace, but more importantly, we will be the peace that meets conflict, violence, and tragedy with hope.

TOPICS FOR DISCUSSION

What Scripture passages come to mind when you think of the ways that our faith comforts us? What Scripture passages speak to you of the necessity of discomfort in the Christian life?

When have you been personally dug up? With others in your group, share what that experience was like.

Talk about how the events of September 11, the war in Iraq, and hurricane Katrina have impacted your spirituality. If possible, get a videotape of the *Frontline* broadcast, "Faith and Doubt at Ground

Zero." Watch a portion of it together and discuss your thoughts and feelings.

Martin Luther King, Jr., said that "true peace is not merely the absence of tension; it is the presence of justice."[11] Discuss this definition of peace.

As a group, write a letter of encouragement to someone from your congregation who is currently serving in the military.

PRAYER AT HOME THIS WEEK

Pray Marcus Borg's prayer (below) over and over again as a means to center yourself. Try to pray the prayer as you go about your everyday tasks this week.

Lord Jesus Christ,
you are the light of the world.
Fill our minds with your peace,
and our hearts with your love.[12]

Questions for journaling:

+ Describe the most peace-filled person that you know.

+ What would it mean for you to be peace in the world?

+ Theologian Emilie Griffin has written that "in prayer we open ourselves to the chance that God will do something that we had not intended."[13] Are you ready to take this risk? Why or why not?

+ Make a list of all of the questions that you have about prayer. How can you begin to explore your questions?

+ The poet George Herbert said that "prayer is the church's banquet."[14] Reflect on this idea in your journal.

Read and meditate on the next section of this study, "Jesus' Prayer Demands Justice."

CORPORATE PRAYER

Have someone sing Malotte's arrangement of Jesus' Prayer in worship this week.

Invite the individuals in your group to write Jesus' Prayer in their own words. Pray the different versions together.

Have a time of "passing the peace" in worship. Explain the significance of this practice.

Pray Carl Micklem's prayer (below) together:

> Show us, good Lord,
> the peace we should seek,
> the peace we must give,
> the peace we can keep,
> the peace we must forgo,
> and the peace you have given in Jesus our Lord.
> Amen.[15]

HYMN SUGGESTIONS

1. "Dona Nobis Pacem"[16]

2. "It Is Well With My Soul"[17]

3. "I've Got Peace Like a River"[18]

4. "Make Me a Channel of Your Peace"[19]

CHAPTER FIVE

~ JESUS' PRAYER DEMANDS JUSTICE

GOD, I WANT TO THANK YOU FOR MY CHURCH—a church that brings meat loaf, mashed potatoes and gravy, green beans, and big pieces of chocolate cake the first Thursday of every month to Supper Club—because this meal brings joy to our neighbor Wilbur, who tells me on the first Wednesday of every month what's coming on the first Thursday. You see, he belongs to a family of big eaters who are also happy on the first Thursday—because they like to sop up that gravy with their bread, so they too are thankful for this meal that gets prayed over by a ten-year-old as everyone waits patiently in line—because she wiggles and giggles and hesitates before she prays, "God is great, God is good, and we thank God for this food, Amen." This prayer, for some odd reason, gets Jacob Reed, who is at the back of the line, to squeeze tears out of his closed eyes—because he once told me he sees God's glory when he stands in line and hears ten-year-olds pray over meat loaf, mashed potatoes and gravy, green beans, and big pieces of chocolate cake.

Personally, I don't see why this man gets all choked up—but then I've never had to stand in line for my only meal of the day—which causes old Jacob Reed to talk in the King James version of the Bible, praising God between the tears and saying, "The Lord doth provideth." I guess he's pretty thankful for this and the ten-year-old and Wilbur's family and meat loaf and especially big pieces of chocolate cake and church members who bring that food thirty miles, all hot and steamy to fill empty stomachs.

So we give thanks tonight for Children and Family Urban Ministries that "doth provideth" for Wilbur and family to eat, for old Jacob Reed to catch a glimpse of the heavenly banquet, for ten-year-olds who giggle through the prayer, and so all of us can experience your kingdom come, your will be done on earth as it is in heaven. With that in mind then, God, all we can say is that You are great, You are good, and we thank You for this food. Amen.[1]

THEOLOGICAL REFLECTION

What does it mean for us who live in a nation of abundance to pray "Give us this day our daily bread"?

We do not pray for "my" bread; it's "our" bread. Bread, after all, is a product of community. We do not eat our bread alone. The farmers in Kansas, the bakers in San

Francisco, the delivery drivers in Detroit, all make bread a cooperative endeavor.

In this nation of unprecedented wealth and resources, substantial numbers of people, many of them children, are hungry and malnourished. The second Food Security Measurement and Research Conference was held February 23–24, 1999, in Alexandria, Virginia. In Session 1 of the conference, Stephen Carlson reported initial U.S. findings: "For the twelve months ending in April 1995, twelve million households . . . experienced some degree of food insecurity. A million of those households . . . experienced either moderate or severe hunger and 800,000 households . . . experienced severe hunger."[2] For the U.S. Department of Agriculture, hunger is an "economic" issue. For Jesus, the issue goes beyond economics; it's an issue of God's justice.

Musa W. Dube Shomana, a lecturer in New Testament at the University of Botswana in Southern Africa, writes: "The Lord's Prayer gives Christian communities and institutions the task of being responsible sons and daughters of God who need to remember those members of the family who do not have any daily bread, but who cannot go on without it. It challenges all who eat, store or throw away food to be producers and givers of daily bread."[3]

To honestly pray "give us this day our daily bread" is to be reminded of our role in establishing God's realm of justice on earth as it is in heaven. It involves feeding the hungry. But there is more to this prayer. It would be an easy task if the prayer were only asking us to share our "leftovers" with those who lack food. The prayer is subversive.

When we pray "our" Father, we are saying that God's life is at the heart of our lives, day after day. We are acknowledging that daily we must reconnect with our God, who gives us the daily bread we need. We are striving to place our complete faith and trust in our Provider.

In the wilderness, the Israelites were grumbling for food. God provided manna and declared with this gift of food, "now you will know that I am the Lord your God."[4] Manna in the desert was not only a sign that God was with them; it also presented a daily test to see if the people could live by trusting God to provide. In fact, the manna rotted after one day. It could not be hoarded. Having an excess of manna was a corruption of the relationship between God and the people.

St. Basil the Great said in a sermon that nothing that belongs to us is ours alone: "The bread that you store up belongs to the hungry; the cloak that lies in your chest belongs to the naked; and the gold that you have hidden in the ground belongs to the poor."[5] Our way of living in this country may prevent us from truly praying the prayer Jesus taught us.

Jesus said, "I am the bread of life."[6] Praying for our daily bread reminds us that those of us who are wealthy by the world's standards must renew our relationship with Jesus, who is truly our "daily bread." We must struggle to follow his way, to speak the truth he spoke, and to live the life he lived. That involves sharing with others in the manner that he shared with us, by spilling his blood for us, by sharing from the essence of his life, by giving of himself without reserve. When we share the deep truth about ourselves, when we share our ignorance and shortcomings, when we share the money we cannot afford to give with those who are in need, then we are beginning to respond to the demand for justice that this prayer presents. The demand for justice placed upon us by this prayer comes to us from Jesus, the very one who died for us.

The theologian Karl Barth said, "To clasp hands in prayer is the beginning of an uprising against the disorder of this world."[7] We must ask ourselves what disorder the prayer disrupts in our world so that God's justice may become reality.

TOPICS FOR DISCUSSION

What does the word "justice" mean to you? How does your faith help you to understand justice?

Micah 6:8 reads: "And what does the Lord require of you but to do justice and to love kindness and to walk humbly with your God." Discuss this scripture passage. How are you striving toward "doing" justice?

What do you mean when you pray, "Give us this day our daily bread"?

What part of your world does Jesus' Prayer disrupt so that God's realm may become reality?

Share a personal experience of Jesus' Prayer demanding justice in a situation in which you found yourself.

PRAYER AT HOME THIS WEEK

Pray Jesus' Prayer every day for the next week.

Read the front page of your newspaper every day this week. Imagine that there is a conversation between the words of Jesus' Prayer and the major news events in the paper. What light does this prayer shed on the issues of the day? Write down your reflections in your journal.

Pray Jesus' Prayer by offering some time this week to volunteer at a local mission or ministry. Reflect upon your experience in light of the words of the prayer.

Find someone in your community who is aware of the basic needs of persons in your community—such as the school principal, a local news reporter, a health-care worker, a beautician, a bartender, a police officer, a pastor. Ask that person to help you identify needs of persons in your community that are not currently being met. Discuss your findings with your study group.

Read and meditate on the next section of this study, "Jesus' Prayer Makes Us One."

CORPORATE PRAYER

Sing together "One Bread, One Body."[8]

Read together the words to "Cuando El Pobre."[9] Pause after each verse and invite the group to reflect on its meaning together.

Obtain a copy of "The Love Feast"[10] and share the service and meal together. Invite members of the group to provide sweet bread for the feast.

Pray the prayer "Bread and Justice":
O God, just as the disciples heard Christ's words of promise and began to eat the bread and drink the wine in the suffering of a long remembrance

and in the joy of a hope, grant that we may hear
your words, spoken in each thing of everyday
affairs:

Coffee, on our table in the morning;
the simple gesture of opening a door to go out,
free;
the shouts of children in the parks;
a familiar song, sung by an unfamiliar face;
a friendly tree that has not yet been cut down.
May simple things speak to us of your mercy, and
tell us that life can be good.

And may these sacramental gifts make us remember those who do not receive them:

who have their lives cut every day, in the bread
absent from the table;
in the door of the hospital, the prison;
the welfare home that does not open;
in sad children, feet without shoes, eyes without
hope;
in war hymns that glorify death;
in deserts where once there was life.
Christ was also sacrificed; and may we learn that
we participate in the saving sacrifice of Christ
when we participate in the suffering of his little
ones. Amen.[11]

Use Jeff Prater's litany *Give Us This Day Our Daily Bread,* Appendix 3, as a closing for your group this week.

HYMN SUGGESTIONS

1. "One Bread, One Body"[12]

2. "For the Healing of the Nations"[13]

3. "Cuando El Pobre" ("When the Poor Ones")[14]

4. "What Does the Lord Require"[15]

CHAPTER SIX

~ JESUS' PRAYER MAKES US ONE

IT WAS SEVERAL YEARS AGO, mid-November, a rainy Saturday afternoon in San Francisco. We had just completed a conference at a large downtown hotel, had walked a bit, and had a cup of cappuccino, when my companion expressed a wish to attend mass. Around the corner was a large Roman Catholic church, just on the edge of Chinatown, with folks of every color and description streaming through the worn oak doors.

Inside, it was easy to imagine some of the dynamics of this congregation. It was, after all, a large downtown church serving a population in transition, struggling to maintain a once ornate building that had housed an affluent congregation, now serving an ethnically and economically diverse and changing community. The ceiling was peeling in places and the carpet was a little worn in spots, but the congregation crowded into the old pews, and folks happily scrunched up to make room for us.

It was an ordinary mass. No special visit from the bishop, no high holy day to celebrate. The scripture for the day was obscure and left me unmoved. The homily was kindly but uninspiring. And then it happened. When it came time for the Jesus' Prayer, the priest invited each person to speak in the language with which they were most comfortable. As I murmured in English, I was surrounded by the sound of the most familiar prayer, prayed in the most intimate fashion, in this most public of places, in how many languages I couldn't even guess. Probably dozens.

I couldn't understand a word of it, yet it was profoundly moving. These words that I did not know were the same ones that I was using. This praying that I did not recognize was the same as my praying. This bread, these trespasses, this temptation, this forgiveness, this God—the same.

In that moment I had an indelible impression of the presence of Jesus Christ in every place, in every person, in every situation, in every country and language that I could imagine. It was like a balloon bursting in my head.

To this day, the memory of that experience—the sound of that prayer—comes back to me often when I pray Jesus' Prayer, even when the only sound I hear is English.[1]

THEOLOGICAL REFLECTION

Jesus' Prayer presumes a community of faith. While the prayer may be used as a part of the individual's private devotion, it oozes with the idea of community and connectedness. It is a prayer learned in community. It is best practiced in community. Its most profound implications are experienced in community.

In Luke's rendering, the prayer is given in response to the disciples' request, "Teach us to pray." Listen to the communal language throughout the prayer: "Our" Father, give "us," forgive "us," lead "us," deliver "us." It may be a cliché, but it is nonetheless true that not once in Jesus' Prayer do you find *I, me,* or *mine.* In a world driven by individualism, consumerism, and self-aggrandizement, this is an important reminder. It is a wake-up call to a church that all too easily has accommodated this cultural encroachment in its quest to be relevant and successful. Prayer should indeed deepen the relationship of the individual to God. Likewise authentic prayer will aid the individual in understanding himself or herself in community—intimately related to sisters and brothers in the faith.

As with most sisters and brothers, we have conflicts among us, and Jesus' Prayer, for all the ways that it unites us, can be one of the sources of conflict. By the time we have prayed only the first two words of the prayer, for example, we have a problem. For some people, the words "our Father" are a profound expression of the intimacy between God and us. For others, the words "our Father" are a painful reminder of an entrenched patriarchy in both church and culture.

This conflict should not and must not be swept aside. How we speak of God, coupled with our earthly relationships, has the power to draw us nearer to the ineffable mystery or to put us at arm's length. Yet, perhaps we spend so much time arguing over the Father language of this prayer that we forget the word that comes before it: "our." This God is "our" God—no matter what language or images we employ, no matter how much we disagree.

In her book, *A Place To Pray: Reflections on the Lord's Prayer,* Roberta Bondi says that the word "our" is one of the most challenging words in the prayer. It means that I am praying to the God of my enemy as well as to the God of my friend.[2] I give up something with the word "our," and I gain something with the word "our." It is a word to usher in the human community, and thus it is a challenging word for each of us.

John Koenig, in referring to intercessory prayer in particular, talks about its capacity "to leap over the fences we humans build between sacred and secular, insiders and outsiders."[3] Jesus' Prayer leaps over the walls of our divisions. It invades our being.

During a regional meeting of United Methodists in Iowa, following a particularly barbed and contentious debate over homosexuality, two people on opposing sides of the issue decided to pray together by walking a labyrinth. Walking slowly, with first one and then the other leading down the narrow path, these two ideological and theological opponents made their way to the center of the labyrinth and to the center of their souls. Afterward they wrote: "Bind us together as only your love can and help us to always remember that our relationship in Christ is first."[4]

In the third century, Bishop Cyprian wrote how the prayer that Jesus taught us does indeed bind us together:

> At some level it doesn't matter whether I think I am praying this prayer alone or whether I consciously acknowledge my basic identity as a member of the body of Christ when I pray it. My unity with other Christians, after all, isn't something I must make happen myself. Whether I want it or not, the fact is that whenever I speak these words, "our Father," "give us . . . our daily bread," by virtue of my very baptism I am praying it as a part of the people of God, and in return they are praying it with me.[5]

Our lack of unity in the church and churches is a source of pain to the heart of God. The call to follow Jesus is a summons to a person and to a particular way of being and doing in the world. A part of that call is to be a sign of the oneness that God intends for us. We may treat unity as an impossible ideal, but it is not an option that the Gospel gives us. Jesus prayed that "they may all be one."[6] We must be the answer to that prayer.

TOPICS FOR DISCUSSION

How does Jesus' Prayer remind you that you are a part of the whole human family?

How does this prayer help you sense your connectedness to other Christians? Discuss the implications of this prayer for private devotions and communal prayer.

Some Christian churches look with suspicion on their members praying with Christians who are not a part of their church family. How do you feel about this?

Could Christians, Muslims, and Jews find shared meaning in praying Jesus' Prayer together?

PRAYER AT HOME THIS WEEK

Each time you pray Jesus' Prayer this week, pause and reflect whenever you get to the word "our" or "us."

In your journal, respond to the following:

+ Where do you see painful divisions in the human family?

+ How does your life and ministry add to those divisions or contribute to their healing?

+ Explore your appreciation for and prejudices toward those who practice the Christian faith differently than you do.

Read and meditate on the next section of this study, "Jesus' Prayer Is Our Life."

CORPORATE PRAYER

Explore using the Korean form of prayer called Tongsung Kido, with everyone praying their individual prayers out loud at the same time.[7]

Make use of Jesus' Prayer in additional languages other than the primary language of your congregation.

Invite a person or persons of a different Christian tradition to talk with you about the meaning of Jesus' Prayer from the perspective of his or her tradition.

Find out what a labyrinth is. See if there is a church in your area that has one. Find persons who will walk it with you. Discuss your experience.

In worship, make use of Evelyn Farnham's litany on Jesus' Prayer, Appendix 4.

HYMN SUGGESTIONS

1. "We Are One in Christ Jesus"[8]

2. "Help Us Accept Each Other"[9]

3. "The Church's One Foundation"[10]

CHAPTER SEVEN

~ JESUS' PRAYER IS OUR LIFE

WHILE I WAS IN AN ALCOHOL TREATMENT center, I had a moving spiritual experience. I had not believed for the last twenty-one years that God would help me. I had not said a single prayer in over twenty years. Why should I pray to an insensitive God who likely isn't there to begin with? God allows Vietnam and racial hatred; why would he care what happens to me—a drunken junkie who had no chances left in life? (I now know that God was working in my life all those years when I distanced myself from him. He made his presence known to me at the treatment center.)

I'd been there detoxing and going to group and reading those stupid, badly written AA books for two or three weeks, and I was about to walk out of treatment. On the night God spoke to me, I was pacing up and down the hall with another guy from Western Nebraska, who was suffering from post-traumatic stress syndrome. I went to my room and lay down on the bed. I grabbed a book called *The Twelve Steps and Twelve Traditions*. The page I opened to was the first step. The book instructed me to pray to God, and even provided the prayer words to use. I decided I'd try it just to prove it didn't work. I went into the bathroom and closed the door. I got down on my knees and prayed the prayer exactly as it was in the book and nothing happened.

Disgusted, I went back to my bed and just lay there. I started to reread the same first page of the first step as I had before praying. It became presently different. The words seemed somehow sacred. I didn't know what was happening, but in spite of my fear I stayed quiet and let the feeling last. Suddenly I felt this feeling of warm water, like a brook or a stream running through me. The light in the room became bright. I felt the warmth and the baptismal cleansing of that moment. I felt my disease washed from my body. A voice inside me said that I would never have to take another drink as long as I lived, as long as I didn't insist on it.

When it was over I was stunned and felt weak. It seemed unlikely that God had spoken to me and healed me, but I could feel it. The compulsion to drink was totally gone. After awhile I went back and looked at the same page. The words were on the page the same as before I prayed. It looked then as it looks now if I read that page—a page in a book again, a page where something powerful and spiritual had happened to me.[1]

THEOLOGICAL REFLECTION

We pray throughout our lives. We look upon the gift of life with all its beauty and fragility, and we say thank you. In the face of death, we dare to pray for strength and comfort. When there is plenty, we pray with grateful hearts. When resources are scarce or even nonexistent, we pray in the hope that our most basic needs will be supplied. When it is well with us we pray, if even less frequently or attentively than we believe we ought. When we are falling apart, like our brother in this week's story, we find words to pray, albeit our fists are pounding, our teeth are clenched, and we declare, "This is the last time." We all pray.

No matter how much we struggle with our inadequacy in prayer, we pray. Even when we think we are not praying, we are. Our praise and our pain directed toward God are indeed prayer. "Prayer is the burden of a sigh, the falling of a tear, the upward glancing of an eye, when none but God is near."[2]

No matter how little or how much we pray, God welcomes the one who leans toward God in prayer. Prayer is so fundamental, so necessary, so shaping, that we are less than we might be without it. The author Anne Lamott is a masterful writer and storyteller. She has a knack for telling it like it is about everyone and everything, including herself. She has known lots of struggle in her life, and she has experienced the awesome power of redemption. She has experienced finding herself, coming home to God, being delivered from lostness. In *Traveling Mercies: Some Thoughts on Faith,* she tells some of her story in poignant vignettes. In one entitled "Why I Make Sam Go to Church," she shares why it is important for her to take her son Sam to church.

> The main reason is that I want to give him what I have found in the world, which is to say a path and a little light to see by. Most of the people I know who have what I want—which is to say, purpose heart, balance, gratitude, joy—are people with a deep sense of spirituality. They are people in community who pray....[3]

Prayer does have the capacity to shape us after the purposes and joys of God. That is why it is so important that we stay at it, no matter how much we anguish over it. We must not let our sense of inadequacy in prayer deter us. And we should not allow puny prayers that lack guts and verve to define us. Martin Luther said to his students, "Oh, if I could only pray the way this dog watches the meat!"[4] Instinctively the dog focuses on the meat because it represents nourishment, strength, and life. Immersing ourselves in prayer can bless us in the same way.

Jesus' Prayer in particular helps us to know our truest needs and to see those needs in the light of God's yearning for the whole creation and us. In Jesus' Prayer, we are asking for great things: for God's realm to come, for forgiveness, for bread for our neighbors and ourselves, and for strength in temptation and adversity. All too often, our own prayers are asking for more baubles and stuff, stuff that will neither satisfy nor last; all of our belongings will ultimately come to rust, rot, and ruin. These things are corruptible. To pray for the great things as we breathe the prayer that Jesus taught us is to join Jesus in praying for that which is incorruptible.

Jesus' Prayer seeks to teach us how to love God and neighbor. In fact, in all of our praying we are striving to love God and love neighbor. We pray Jesus' Prayer in our solitude and in community until we become the prayer, so internalizing the words that they become us and we become them.

One wise preacher once said, "If I can't sing, I can't pray. And if I can't pray, I can't breathe. And if I can't breathe, I'm not alive."[5] Jesus' Prayer is our life. Jesus' Prayer gives us life. Jesus' Prayer leads us to the life eternal—to the kingdom and the power and the glory of our God. Amen.

TOPICS FOR DISCUSSION

How does prayer give you life?

How has focusing on Jesus' Prayer enriched your prayer life? How have you been challenged in your faith?

What is your most important learning from this study?

Has this study generated any new ministry ideas for you? For your church?

PRAYER AT HOME THIS WEEK

In your journal, respond to the following:

+ Name your spiritual hungers.

+ What holy habits nourish you?

+ What is the next step for you in your life of prayer?

CORPORATE PRAYER

As a study group, share Holy Communion or a Love Feast.[6]

HYMN SUGGESTIONS

Please select similar hymns that may be found in your denominational hymn book or select other similar songs.

1. "Jesus Remember Me"[7]

2. "Prayer Is the Soul's Sincere Desire"[8]

3. "Kum Ba Yah"[9]

4. "Sweet Hour of Prayer"[10]

~ ONLY AS WE FORGIVE [1]

An open letter to an arsonist,

It was September 14, 2000. You drove down the gravel road that leads to our small country church about five miles from Indianola. It must have been a little after 4 AM, the darkest part of the night, when you kicked in the basement window under our 107-year-old sanctuary. I know you poured gasoline into the basement and struck a match. I don't know if you stayed and watched the destruction that you caused. I don't know if you intended to harm our community in particular or perhaps the church in general. Maybe you were mad at God or your parents. You may have been too stoned to know how wrong it was. I don't know.

In some ways it is hard to believe that two years have passed. Most Sundays you could have found us at worship in Smith Chapel on the campus of Simpson College. On Christmas Eve, we worshiped outside next to the hole that was left when they removed the charred remains of our building. It was cold, so we lit a fire. It's strange. The fire that night burned a brilliant orange just like yours. We stood holding each other as we watched the flames move just like we did that night in September. The wind was howling, but we managed to hear words from the Christmas story. We heard words like "fear not" and "a light shines in the darkness and the darkness did not overcome it." No, the fire we lit that night brought us some comfort; yours brought us only pain.

You probably do not know just how much pain you inflicted on us as a community. Or how hard it was to drive by that gaping hole that once cradled our house of worship. The pain took many forms. Sometimes many forms in the span of a single day. The pain has been a companion of sorts, some days more obvious than others. Perhaps you know something about pain. Maybe that is why you broke the window and struck the match, I don't know.

On the one-year anniversary of your fire, we gathered like we did on Christmas Eve. It was three days after the September 11 attacks, so we had our nation's grief layered on top of our own. This time we went down into the hole. We sang and we prayed. Then we heard these words from Psalm 130.

Out of the depths I cry to you, O Lord. Hear my voice.

Let your ears be attentive to the voice of my supplications.

If you, O Lord, should mark iniquities, who could stand?

But there is forgiveness with you.

I wait for the Lord, my soul waits, and in God's word I hope.

We will not have to wait much longer for our new building to be completed. The process to design and build a church has been lengthy, but we feel good about what we have been able to accomplish. The hole was filled in. We will plant a garden where our old building once stood. The new building sits just off to the side, and you will recognize some of the features from the one you burned. Our worship time is 9 AM every Sunday. I tell you this because I want you to know that you are invited. In fact, we even plan to reserve a seat just for you. Our faith has a lot to say about forgiveness. Every Sunday we ask God to forgive our sins but only as we have forgiven those who have sinned against us. That would be you. So if you would join us for worship, we could practice this kind of forgiveness face to face. I say "practice" for a reason. I don't expect us to get it right the first or even the second time.

Of course we'll continue to work to forgive you even if you decline our invitation to worship. Forgiveness is the cornerstone of the faith we have inherited. Some people think it is impossible. They may be right. I only know that we have to try. Our forgiveness of you is tied to God's forgiveness of us. We can't receive something we are not willing to give to others. So you see, if we harbor hatred for you in our hearts, we harbor smoldering ashes of your arson. If we cling to bitterness, we fan the embers of your violent act. If we fantasize about revenge, we rekindle a destructive flame that will consume us. Forgiveness may indeed be impossible, but for us it is not optional.

Wherever you are, whoever you are, you remain in our prayers.

Sincerely,
Rev. Ted Lyddon Hatten

~ Jesus' Prayer in Hymns [1]

OUR FATHER WHO ART IN HEAVEN

This is my Father's world, and to my listening ears
All nature sings, and round me rings the music of the
spheres.
This is my Father's world: I rest me in the thought
Of rocks and trees, of skies and seas; His hand the
wonders wrought.

This is my Father's world, the birds their carols raise,
The morning light, the lily white, declare their maker's
praise.
This is my Father's world: He shines in all that's fair,
In the rustling grass, I hear Him pass; He speaks to me
everywhere.[2]

HALLOWED BE THY NAME

Holy, holy, holy! Lord God Almighty!
Early in the morning, we praise your majesty.
Holy, holy, holy! Merciful and mighty,
God in three persons, blessed Trinity!
Holy, holy, holy! Though we know but dimly,

Though the eye of humankind, your glory may not see,
You alone are holy, you alone are worthy,
Perfect in power, in love and purity.[3]

THY KINGDOM COME

Rejoice, give thanks and sing; your Sovereign God
adore!
For Christ has robbed death's sting and triumphs ever-
more.
Lift up your heart, life up your voice;
Rejoice; again I say, rejoice.[4]

THY WILL BE DONE ON EARTH AS IT IS IN HEAVEN

Seek ye first the kingdom of God and His righteousness,
And all these things shall be added unto you.
Allelu, alleluia!
Ask, and it shall be given unto you; seek and ye shall
find;
Knock, and the door shall be opened unto you.
Allelu, alleluia![5]

GIVE US THIS DAY OUR DAILY BREAD

As the sun doth daily rise,
Brightening all the morning skies,
So to thee with one accord
Lift we up our hearts, O Lord.

Day by day provide us food,
For from thee come all things good;
Strength unto our souls afford
From thy living bread, O Lord.[6]

AND FORGIVE US OUR TRESPASSES AS WE FORGIVE THOSE WHO TRESPASS AGAINST US

"Forgive our sins as we forgive,"
You taught us, Lord, to pray;
But you alone can grant us grace
To live the words we say.
Lord, cleanse the depths within our souls,
And bid resentment cease;
Then, bound to all in bonds of love,
Our lives will spread your peace.[7]

AND LEAD US NOT INTO TEMPATION, BUT DELIVER US FROM EVIL

I want a principle within of watchful, godly fear,
A sensibility of sin, a pain to feel it near.
I want the first approach to feel of pride or wrong
desire,
To catch the wandering of my will, and quench the
kindling fire.
From thee that I no more may stray, no more thy
goodness grieve,

Grant me the filial awe, I pray, the tender conscience give.

Quick as the apple of an eye, O God, my conscience make;

Awake my soul when sin is nigh, and keep it still awake.[8]

FOR THINE IS THE KINGDOM, AND THE POWER, AND THE GLORY FOREVER

Praise, my soul, the King of heaven, to the throne thy tribute bring;

Ransomed, healed, restored, forgiven

Evermore God's praises sing.

Alleluia! Alleluia! Praise the everlasting King.

Praise the Lord for grace and favor to all people in distress;

Praise God, still the same as ever,

Slow to chide, swift to bless.

Alleluia! Alleluia! Glorious now God's faithfulness.[9]

AMEN

Alleluia, He's my Savior, Alleluia, He's my Savior

Alleluia, He's my Savior, Alleluia, alleluia.

Alleluia, I will praise Him, Alleluia, I will praise Him

Alleluia, I will praise Him, Alleluia, alleluia.[10]

~ GIVE US THIS DAY OUR DAILY BREAD

Lord,
We are such hungry people.

Give us this day our daily bread.

We hunger for food,
for acceptance,
for love.

Give us this day our daily bread.
Lord, we hunger for mercy and truth,
for righteousness
and simplicity of heart.

Give us this day our daily bread.

Lord, we hunger for forgiveness,
for enlightenment,
for holy vision,
for peace.
Give us this day our daily bread.

We hunger in hope…
for the needy,
for the downtrodden and forgotten,
for the weak,
for ourselves.
Lord,
We are such a hungry people.

Give us this day our daily bread.

~ Litany on Jesus' Prayer [1]

Leader:	Our Father in Heaven, hallowed be your name—the prayer that is always worshipful, the prayer that is always reverent.
People:	**As we pray this prayer, not once do we say "I."**
Leader:	Your kingdom come, your will be done on earth as it is in heaven—the prayer that is always assuring, the prayer that is always trusting.
People:	**In praying the Lord's prayer, never do we say "my."**
Leader:	Give us this day our daily bread—the prayer that is always sufficient to our needs, the prayer that is always faithful.
People:	**And when we ask for daily bread, we must include our sisters and brothers.**

Leader: Forgive us our sins as we forgive those who sin against us—the prayer that is always compassionate, the prayer that is always filled with grace.

People: **When we pray the Lord's prayer, we pray for one another.**

Leader: Save us from the time of trial and deliver us from evil—the prayer that is always liberating, the prayer that is always all-encompassing.

People: **For others are included in each and every plea. From the beginning to the end, it does not once say "me."**

Leader: For the Kingdom, the power, and the glory are yours forever and evermore—the prayer that is always new, the prayer that is always steadfast, the prayer that is always constant.

People: **AMEN and AMEN!!**

~ Notes

Chapter 1:
Jesus' Prayer Opens Us to the Holy

1. This story was submitted by Connie Zeleney, St. Paul United Methodist Church, La Porte City, Iowa.

2. Lucy Maud Montgomery, *Anne of Green Gables* (Philadelphia: Running, 1993), 74.

3. Roberta Bondi, *A Place to Pray: Reflections on the Lord's Prayer* (Nashville: Abingdon, 1998), 12.

4. Richard Foster, *Prayer: Finding the Heart's True Home* (San Francisco: Harper, 1992), 3.

5. This story was submitted by the Reverend Hal Green, Wesley United Methodist Church, Muscatine, Iowa.

6. Walt Whitman, *The Poetry and Prose of Walt Whitman* (New York: Simon and Schuster, 1949), 139.

7. Doris Grumbach, *The Presence of Absence: On Prayers and an Epiphany* (Boston: Beacon, 1998), 74.

8. *The United Methodist Hymnal: Book of United Methodist Worship* (Nashville: United Methodist Publishing House, 1989), 271 (hereafter referred to as *U.M. Hymnal*).

9. Ibid., 493; John W. Peterson and Norman Johnson, comp., and Norman Johnson, ed., *Praise! Our Songs and Hymns* (Grand Rapids: Songspiration Music, 1979), 422 (hereafter referred to as Peterson, *Praise!*).

10. *U.M. Hymnal,* 358; Peterson, *Praise!,* 406; *The Hymnal 1982* (New York: *Church Hymnal,* 1982), 652–53 (hereafter referred to as *Hymnal* [1982]); *The Lutheran Book of Worship* (Minneapolis: Augsburg, 1995), 506; *The Presbyterian*

Hymnal: Hymns, Psalms, and Spiritual Songs (Louisville: Westminster John Knox, 1990), 345 (hereafter referred to as *Presbyterian Hymnal*); *The New Century Hymnal* (Cleveland: The Pilgrim Press, 1995), 502.

11. *The Faith We Sing*, pew ed. (Nashville: Abingdon Press, 2000), 2025.

12. Ibid., 2086.

Chapter 2:
Jesus' Prayer Teaches the Faith

1. This story was submitted by The Reverend Mary Alice Gran, director of Children's Ministries, General Board of Discipleship, Nashville, Tennessee.

2. Luke 11: 1.

3. Michael Crosby, *The Prayer that Jesus Taught Us* (Maryknoll: Orbis, 2002), 4.

4. This story was submitted by Maureen Williams, Fifth Avenue United Methodist Church, Council Bluffs, Iowa.

5. This story was submitted by Allen Anneberg, Carroll United Methodist Church, Carroll, Iowa.

6. Luke 10: 27.

7. *U.M. Hymnal,* 570.

8. Ibid., 292; Robert J. Batastini, ed., *Gather: Comprehensive,* 2d ed. (Chicago: GIA, 1998), 614; *The Hymnal 1982,* 439; *Lutheran Book of Worship,* 385; *Presbyterian Hymnal,* 85; *Singing the Living Tradition* (Unitarian Universalist Association, Boston: Beacon Press, 1993), 18; *New Century Hymnal,* 223.

9. *Faith We Sing,* 2223; Batastani, *Gather,* 728.

10. *U.M. Hymnal,* 405; Peterson, *Praise!,* 438; Batastini, *Gather,* 600; *The Hymnal* (1982), 711; *With One Voice: A Lutheran Resource for Worship* (Minneapolis: Augsburg Fortress, 2001), 783; *Presbyterian Hymnal,* 333.

11. *U.M. Hymnal,* 402; Peterson, *Praise!,* 381; *Presbyterian Hymnal,* 372; *New Century Hymnal,* 454.

12. *Faith We Sing,* 2236; Batastani, *Gather,* 743; *With One Voice,* 718.

Chapter 3:
Jesus' Prayer Calls Us to Forgiveness

1. This story was submitted by Kathleen Marvin, Onawa United Methodist Church, Onawa, Iowa.

2. John Koenig, *Rediscovering New Testament Prayer: Boldness and Blessing in the Name of Jesus* (Harrisburg: Morehouse Publishing, 1992), 103.

3. Romans 7: 19.

4. George Appleton, ed., *The Oxford Book of Prayer* (New York: Oxford University Press, 1985), 108.

5. Luke 23: 34.

6. Coretta Scott King, ed., *The Words of Martin Luther King, Jr.* (New York: Newmarket, 1983), 23.

7. This story was submitted by the Reverend Ted Lyddon Hatten, Farmers Chapel United Methodist Church, Indianola, Iowa.

8. Desmond Tutu, *No Future Without Forgiveness* (New York: Doubleday, 1999).

9. Michael Counsell, ed., *2000 Years of Prayer* (Harrisburg: Morehouse, 1999), 469.

10. Emilie Griffin, *Clinging: The Experience of Prayer* (New York: McCracken, 1994), 13.

11. *Faith We Sing,* 2278; Batastani, *Gather,* 7, 15, 150; *Presbyterian Hymnal,* 571, 589, 590.

12. *U.M. Hymnal,* 390; Batastani, *Gather,* 848; *Hymnal* (1982), 674; *With One Voice,* 307; *Presbyterian Hymnal,* 347.

13. *U.M. Hymnal,* 618; Peterson, *Praise!,* 162; Batastani, *Gather,* 832; *Hymnal* (1982), 325; *Lutheran Book of Worship,* 212; *Presbyterian Hymnal,* 513; *Singing the Living Tradition,* 406; *New Century Hymnal,* 330.

14. *U.M. Hymnal,* 623; Peterson, *Praise!,* 157; *Hymnal* (1982), 318; *With One Voice,* 211.

Chapter 4:
Jesus' Prayer Brings Us Peace

1. This story was submitted by the Reverend Don Hodson, Salem United Methodist Church, Cedar Rapids, Iowa.

2. This reflection was submitted

by a high school student who wishes to remain anonymous.

3. This reflection was submitted by Lindsey Beglinger, Collegiate United Methodist Church, Ames, Iowa.

4. This reflection was submitted by Paul McKinley, Friendship Haven, Fort Dodge, Iowa.

5. Mark 4: 39.

6. This story was submitted by the Reverend Mary Green, Eagle Grove United Methodist Church, Eagle Grove, Iowa.

7. *Faith and Doubt at Ground Zero* (Boston: Frontline, 2002).

8. John 14: 27

9. This reflection was submitted by Bishop James S. Thomas, Bishop of the Iowa Annual Conference of the United Methodist Church from 1964–76.

10. Appleton, ed., *Oxford Book of Prayer,* 88–89.

11. King, ed., *Words of Martin Luther King, Jr.,* 83.

12. Marcus Borg, "What is Faith?"[sermon on-line]; available from

http://www.explorefaith.org/LentenHomily03.16.01.html; Internet.

13. Griffin, *Clinging,* 5.

14. George Herbert, "Prayer," *The Works of George Herbert,* ed. F. E. Hutchinson (Oxford: Clarendon Press, 1945), 51.

15. Appleton, ed., *Oxford Book of Prayer,* 80.

16. *U.M. Hymnal,* 376; Batastani, *Gather,* 724; *Hymnal* (1982), 712; *With One Voice,* 774; *Singing the Living Tradition,* 388.

17. *U.M. Hymnal,* 377; Peterson, *Praise!,* 321.

18. *Faith We Sing,* 2145; Peterson, *Praise!,* 345; *Presbyterian Hymnal,* 368; *Singing the Living Tradition,* 100; *New Century Hymnal,* 478.

19. *The Faith We Sing,* 2171; Batastani, *Gather,* 721.

Chapter 5:
Jesus' Prayer Demands Justice
1. This prayer was given by The Reverend Denny Coon before a banquet that celebrated the tenth anniversary of

Children and Family Urban Ministries, housed at Trinity United Methodist Church, Des Moines, Iowa.

2. Margaret S. Andrews and Mark A. Prell, *Second Food Security Measurement and Research Conference,* Volume 1: *Proceedings: Food Assistance and Nutrition Research Report No. (FANRR-11-1): Overview* (Economic Research Service/USDA, 2001 [cited 3 June 2005]); available from http://www.ers.usda.gov/publications/Fanrr11-1.

3. Crosby, *The Prayer that Jesus Taught Us,* 119.

4. Exodus 16: 12

5. *The World Treasury of Religious Quotations,* compiled and edited by Ralph L. Woods (N.Y.: Hawthorn Books, 1966).

6. John 6: 35

7. Jann Cather Weaver and Roger Wedell, *Imaging the Word: An Arts and Lectionary Resource,* vol. 1, ed. Kenneth Lawrence (Cleveland: United Church Press, 1994), 229.

8. *U.M. Hymnal,* 620;

Batastani, *Gather,* 813; *With One Voice,* 710.

9. *U.M. Hymnal,* 434; *Presbyterian Hymnal,* 407.

10. *The United Methodist Book of Worship,* 581.

11. *U.M. Hymnal,* 639.

12. Ibid., 620; Batastani, *Gather,* 813; *With One Voice,* 710.

13. *U.M. Hymnal,* 428; Batastani, *Gather,* 712; *New Century Hymnal,* 476.

14. *U.M.,* 434; *Presbyterian Hymnal,* 407.

15. *U.M. Hymnal,* 441; *Hymnal* (1982), 605; *Presbyterian Hymnal,* 405.

Chapter 6:
Jesus' Prayer Makes Us One

1. This story was submitted by Twila Glen, Grace United Methodist Church, Des Moines, Iowa.

2. Bondi, *A Place to Pray,* 29.

3. Koenig, *Rediscovering New Testament Prayer,* 81.

4. Jeff Kodis and Bill Crews, June 8, 1998, in a journal left beside the labyrinth.

5. Bondi, *A Place to Pray,* 27.

6. John 17: 21

7. *United Methodist Book of Worship,* 446.

8. *The Faith We Sing,* 2229.

9. *U.M. Hymnal,* 560; *Hymnal* (1982), 525; *Presbyterian Hymnal,* 358; *New Century Hymnal,* 388.

10. *U.M.Hymnal,* 546; *Lutheran Book of Worship,* 369; *New Century Hymnal,* 386.

Chapter 7:
Jesus' Prayer Is Our Life

1. This story was submitted by an anonymous recovering alcoholic.

2. *U.M. Hymnal,* 492; *New Century Hymnal,* 508.

3. Anne Lamott, *Traveling Mercies: Some Thoughts on Faith* (New York: Pantheon, 1999), 100.

4. Martin Luther, *Luther's Works,* Vol. 54 (Philadelphia: Fortress, 1967), 38.

5. Anonymous

6. *U.M. Hymnal,* 12–15; Theology and Worship Ministry Unit, *The Book of Common Worship,* pastoral ed. (Louisville: Westminster, 1998), 291–99.

7. *U.M. Hymnal,* 488; Batastani, *Gather,* 422; *With One Voice,* 740; *Presbyterian Hymnal,* 599.

8. *U.M.Hymnal,* 492; *New Century Hymnal,* 508.

9. *U.M. Hymnal,* 494; *Presbyterian Hymnal,* 338; *Singing the Living Tradition,* 401.

10. *U.M. Hymnal,* 496; Peterson, *Praise!,* 414; *New Century Hymnal,* 505.

~ Notes to Appendixes
Appendix 1:
Only as We Forgive

1. This was submitted by the Reverend Ted Lyddon Hatten, Farmers Chapel and Center Chapel United Methodist Churches, Indianola, Iowa.

Appendix 2:
Jesus' Prayer in Hymns

1. This was submitted by Jean Humphrey, Collegiate United Methodist Church, Wesley Foundation, Ames, Iowa.

2. *U.M. Hymnal,* 144; Peterson, *Praise!,* 56; *The Hymnal* (1982), 651; *Lutheran Book of Worship,* 554; *Presbyterian Hymnal,* 293.

3. *U.M. Hymnal,* 64; Peterson, *Praise!,* 41;. Batastini, *Gather,* 483; *Hymnal* (1982), 362; *Lutheran Book of Worship,* 165; *Presbyterian Hymnal,* 580; *New Century Hymnal,* 277.

4. *U.M. Hymnal,* 715; Peterson, *Praise!,* 245; Batastini, *Gather,* 493; *Hymnal* (1982), 481; *Lutheran Book of Worship,* 171; *Presbyterian Hymnal,* 155; *New Century Hymnal,* 303.

5. *U.M. Hymnal,* 405; Peterson, *Praise!,* 438; Batastini, *Gather,* 600; *Hymnal* (1982), 711; *With One Voice,* 783; *Presbyterian Hymnal,* 333.

6. *U.M. Hymnal,* 675.

7. Ibid., 390; Batastini, *Gather,* 848; *Hymnal* (1982), 674; *Lutheran Book of Worship,* 307; *Presbyterian Hymnal,* 347.

8. *U.M. Hymnal,* 410.

9. Ibid., 66; Peterson, *Praise!,* 52; Batastini, *Gather,* 531; *Hymnal* (1982), 410; *Lutheran Book of Worship,* 549; *Presbyterian Hymnal,* 479.

10. *U.M. Hymnal,* 186; Peterson, *Praise!,* 30.

Appendix 3:
Give Us This Day Our Daily Bread

1. This was submitted by Dr. Jeffrey Prater, Collegiate United Methodist Church, Wesley Foundation, Ames, Iowa.

Appendix 4:
Litany on Jesus' Prayer

1. This was submitted by Evelyn Farnham, Gowrie United Methodist Church, Gowrie, Iowa.

~ BIBLIOGRAPHY

Appleton, George, ed. *The Oxford Book of Prayer.* New York: Oxford University Press, 1985.

Barclay, William. *The Lord's Prayer.* Louisville: Westminster, 1999.

Bondi, Roberta C. *A Place to Pray: Reflections on the Lord's Prayer.* Nashville: Abingdon, 1998.

————. *To Pray and to Love: Conversations on Prayer with the Early Church.* Minneapolis: Fortress, 1991.

Crosby, Michael H. *The Prayer that Jesus Taught Us.* Maryknoll: Orbis, 2002.

Edwards, Tilden. *Living in the Presence: Disciplines for the Spiritual Heart.* San Francisco: Harper, 1987.

Ebeling, Gerhard. *Lord's Prayer.* Orleans, Mass.: Paraclete, 2000.

Foster, Richard. *Prayer: Finding the Heart's Home.* San Francisco: Harper, 1992.

Griffin, Emilie. *Clinging: The Experience of Prayer.* New York: McCracken, 1994.

————. *Doors into Prayer: An Invitation.* Orleans, Mass.: Paraclete, 2001.

Hallesby, Ole. *Prayer.* Minneapolis: Augsburg, 1994.

Häring, Bernard. *Our Father.* Trans. by Gwen Griffith-Dickson. Winona: St. Mary's, 1995.

Jeremias, Joachim. *The Lord's Prayer.* Minneapolis: Fortress, 1964.

Job, Rueben P. *A Guide to Prayer for All God's People.* Nashville: Upper Room, 1990.

Keating, Thomas. *Active Meditation for Contemplative Prayer.* New York: Continuum, 1997.

Killinger, John. *Beginning Prayer.* Nashville: Upper Room, 1993.

Koenig, John. *Rediscovering New Testament Prayer: Boldness and Blessing in the Name of Jesus.* Harrisburg: Morehouse, 1992.

Lamott, Anne. *Traveling Mercies: Some Thoughts on Faith.* New York: Pantheon, 1999.

Mathias, Philip. *Perfect Prayer.* Minneapolis: Augsburg, 2004.

Migliore, Daniel L. *The Lord's Prayer: Perspectives for Reclaiming Christian Prayer.* Grand Rapids: Erdmans, 1993.

Mother Teresa, and Brother Roger. *Seeking the Heart of God: Reflections on Prayer.* San Francisco: Harper, 1991.

Mother Teresa. *For God: A Yearbook of Prayers and Meditations.* Comp. Angelo D. Scolozzi. Cincinnati, Ohio: St. Anthony Messenger, 2000.

Mulholland, James R. *Praying Like Jesus: The Lord's Prayer in a Culture of Prosperity.* San Francisco: Harper, 2001.

Muller, Wayne. *Learning to Pray: How We Find Heaven on Earth.* New York: Bantam, 2004.

Nouwen, Henri. *The Way of the Heart.* New York: Ballantine, 1981.

Paton, Alan. *Instrument of Thy Peace: Meditations on the Prayer of St. Francis of Assisi.* New York: Seabury, 1982.

Steere, Douglas. *Dimensions of Prayer: Cultivating a Relationship with God.* Nashville: Upper Room, 1962.

Stevenson, Kenneth W. *Lord's Prayer: Text in Tradition.* Minneapolis: Augsburg, 2004.

Teresa of Avila. *The Way of Perfection.* Trans. E. Allison Peers. New York: Doubleday, 1989.

The United Methodist Hymnal. Nashville: United Methodist House, 1989.

Willimon, William H., and Stanley Hauerwas. *Lord, Teach Us: The Lord's Prayer and the Christian Life.* Nashville: Abingdon, 1996.